MW01347706

Trey

Happy 14th Birthday

Love always,
Your Nana

Made in the USA
Middletown, DE
09 August 2020

14641379R00066